Published by:
Zoe Life Publishing
P.O. Box 871066
Canton, MI 48187 USA

Author: Joshua Johnson
Illustrator: Joshua Johnson
Editor: Colleen Wilson

First U.S. Edition 2006
Publisher's Cataloging-In-Publication Data

Johnson, Joshua

When a Kid Dreams

Summary: Illustrated, poetic adventures of childhood dreams

10 Digit ISBN 0-9748251-9-0 Soft Cover Edition
13 Digit ISBN: 978-974251-9-9 Soft Cover Edition

1. Children / youth poetry (age 8 and up)

Library of Congress Control Number: 2006921770

For current information about releases by Joshua Johnson or other releases from Zoe Life Publishing, visit our web site: http://www.zoelifepub.com

Printed in the United States of America

When A Kid Dreams

The illustrated poetry of

Joshua Johnson

Zoe Life Publishing

Contents of a dream . . .

When A Kid Dreams

Everyone Wins

When Inspiration Gets Out

The Day Inspiration Got Out . . .

In middle school I had a teacher, Dr. Thomas Blackwell, who encouraged my peers and I to recite famous quotes. Of all the quotes, one really puzzled me. "The Strangest Secret: You become what you think about," by Earl Nightingale.

About ten years later I began to search my cardboard box full of old artifacts. I found my folder from Dr. Blackwell's famous quotes.
I thought about my thirteen year old mentality. I learned that at some point I had forgotten my childhood dreams.

I continued to search my old belongings until I came across something that would change my life. I found an employment application that Dr. Blackwell demanded his students to observe and complete.
I was inspired to notice that for college education, I had written in the University of Michigan. My first year at the University of Michigan had just come to an end. I had accomplished a great dream while stumbling into The Strangest Secret: You become what you think about.

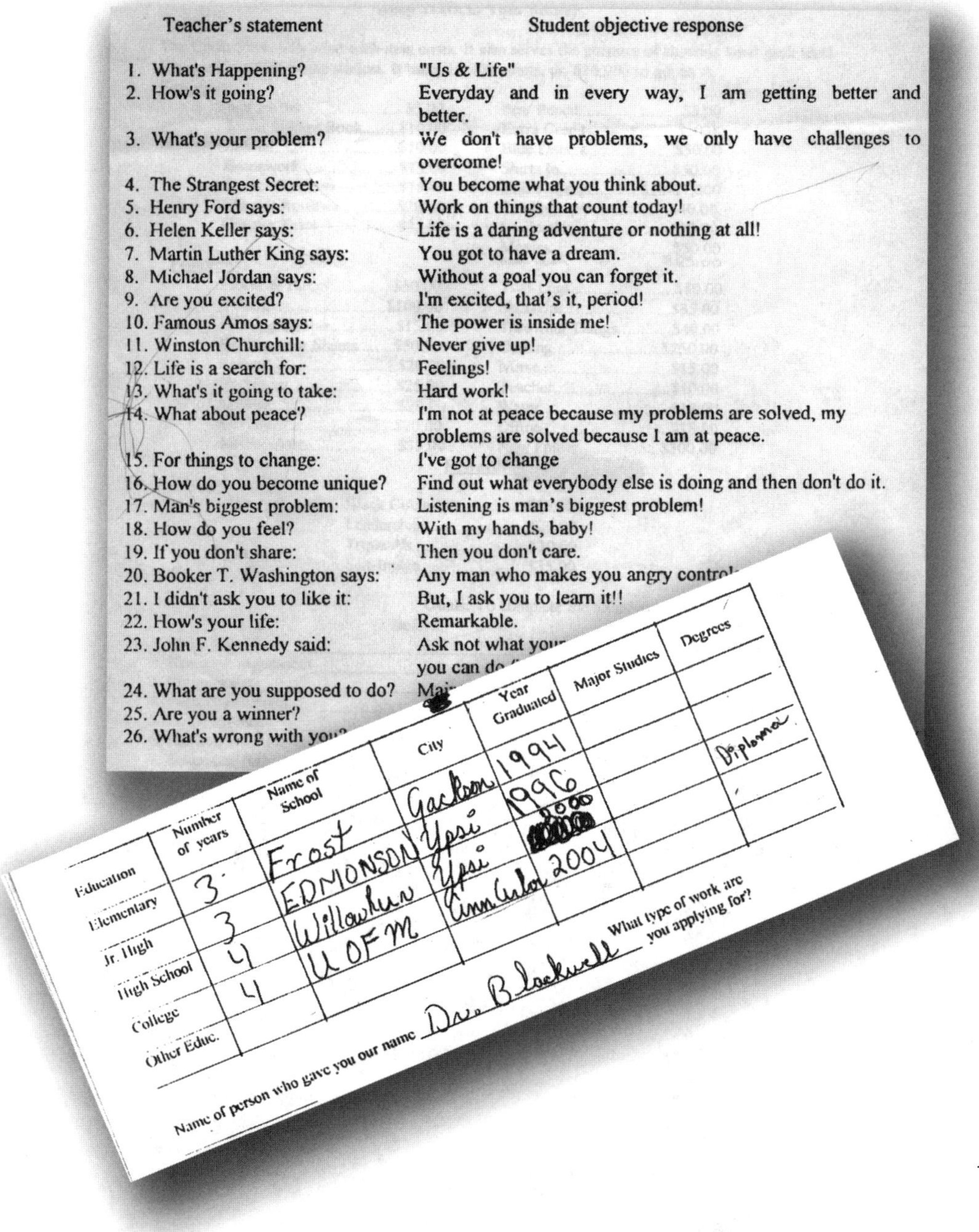

Teacher's statement	Student objective response
1. What's Happening?	"Us & Life"
2. How's it going?	Everyday and in every way, I am getting better and better.
3. What's your problem?	We don't have problems, we only have challenges to overcome!
4. The Strangest Secret:	You become what you think about.
5. Henry Ford says:	Work on things that count today!
6. Helen Keller says:	Life is a daring adventure or nothing at all!
7. Martin Luther King says:	You got to have a dream.
8. Michael Jordan says:	Without a goal you can forget it.
9. Are you excited?	I'm excited, that's it, period!
10. Famous Amos says:	The power is inside me!
11. Winston Churchill:	Never give up!
12. Life is a search for:	Feelings!
13. What's it going to take:	Hard work!
14. What about peace?	I'm not at peace because my problems are solved, my problems are solved because I am at peace.
15. For things to change:	I've got to change
16. How do you become unique?	Find out what everybody else is doing and then don't do it.
17. Man's biggest problem:	Listening is man's biggest problem!
18. How do you feel?	With my hands, baby!
19. If you don't share:	Then you don't care.
20. Booker T. Washington says:	Any man who makes you angry control
21. I didn't ask you to like it:	But, I ask you to learn it!!
22. How's your life:	Remarkable.
23. John F. Kennedy said:	Ask not what your you can do
24. What are you supposed to do?	Ma
25. Are you a winner?	
26. What's wrong with you?	

Education	Number of years	Name of School	City	Year Graduated	Major Studies	Degrees
Elementary	3	Frost	Jackson	1994		
Jr. High	3	EDMONSON	Ypsi	1996		
High School	4	Willowrun	Ypsi	[illegible]		Diploma
College	4	U OF M	Ann Arbor	2004		
Other Educ.						

What type of work are you applying for?

Name of person who gave you our name Dr. Blackwell

Thanks...

On my humblest day I write to say
I give much thanks to you.
You believed in me
long enough to see,
"The little kid's dream came true!"

If anyone questions the struggles
may they search my laundry for proof.
They'll know of all my challenges
full of support from you.

Connie and Larry Clifton
Margaret and Charles Johnson
Asenath and Ralph Johnson
Kathe Rogers
Sabrina and Brian Adams
Jeanne Weinch
Fred Horowitz
Earl Jackson
John Megahan
Kenya
Philip Lloyd
Bill Burgard
Ralph, Mark, Jeremiah
Robert Lucas
Alexandra McCracken
Martha, Shavon, Bryant
Christine Wylie
Gloria Taylor
Darlene Rankins
Theda Gibbs
Brian Banks
Johnson and Turner Family
Gail Brooks
Benita Matthews
Hannah Smotrich
Colleen Wilson

And everyone else!

4 My Greatest Dream Ever;
The Light Of My World

It's okay to smile when a kid dreams,
because everyone wins when inspiration gets out...

Welcome

Please do come inside.
Well, I hope that you'll learn.
I'm sure you're quite skeptical and merely concerned.
We all are suspicious so discover the "what."
Here are a few words you can feel free to eat up.

Is it Good or Bad food?
It depends on your acquire.
Unbolt your mind so opinions can transpire.
Take your spoons and scoop a page or two.
Pages turned quickly may not be for you.
But
if the taste is great and your stomach's lean,
continue to read and enjoy your dreams.

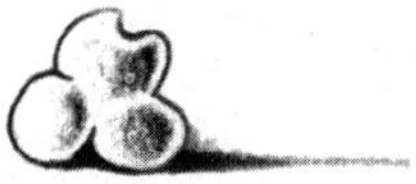

It's Okay To Smile

The Rolling Coaster

I'll tell you about a roller coaster that never came back.
Anxiously in line, I waved my hat.
Everyone watched the coaster skulk up the first hill
until all that was seen was a spark of the wheel.

Back in sight the coaster plunged from its peak
with record breaking speed leaving bright blue streaks.
The riders were laughing, but holding on tight.
They seemed to be having the time of their lives.
Flying up the last hill they shot from the track.
I waited,
but the roller coaster never came back.

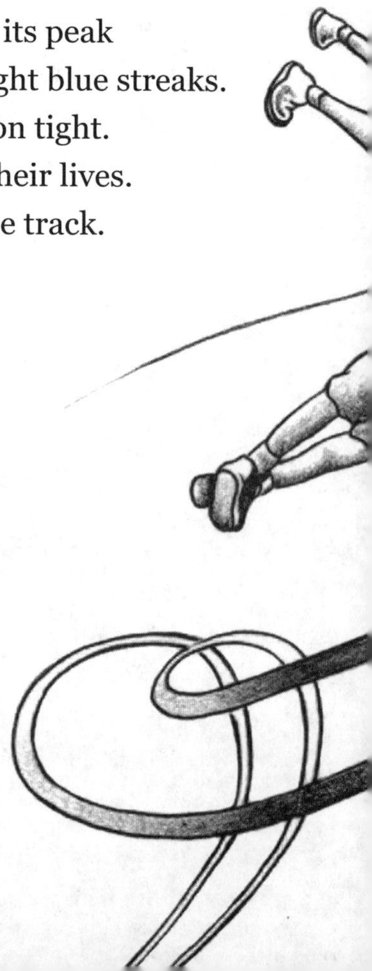

Bicycling in the Woods

My daddy taught me to be very observant
when bicycling in the woods:

He said, "Honey look out for wild dogs!"
  "Be sure to watch out for bees!"
But poor simple dad,
how could this be?
  He never mentioned the trees!

Danny's Stuck in the Tree!

Danny was stuck in a tree,
a tree from which he couldn't get down.
I ran around town and surprisingly found
a red haired, blue-eyed clown.

I approached the tree with the clown and his glee
he unleashed his funniest of jokes.
Danny almost laughed the tree in half
as the branch he hung from broke.

That day the whole town believed,
even a clown can do a good deed.

Mom's an ATM

Mom's an ATM.
She always gives me money.
Sometimes she'll play and say she's broke,
and I don't find it funny.

I push Mom's buttons,
and if I have to I'll pout
until I'm granted her palms to take money out.
Banking is simple when using "Mom's card."
Especially since the maximum seems so far.

Most ATM's are stationary, but mine's quite mobile.
She brings a stash of cash
each time I'm in trouble.
I try to stay away from the daily limit,
though that's a hard task when shopping's so splendid.

When Mom says, "That's it!" It's time to pause,
keeping track of previous deposits and withdrawls.
Mom gets paid on Wednesday's and a bonus on Friday's.
So Tuesday's and Thursday's are the perfect, "Hi!" days.

My friends say I'm spoiled,
but I don't need them.
All I need is my mom,
since she's my ATM.

Mr. Snail and the Whale

At the well was Mr. Snail who lost his nails.
He used a pail to retrieve them.
Up came the pail half-eaten by a Whale, hoping
Mr. Snail would slither down to meet him.

No One Chews Like Betsie Bleu

Betsie Bleu, she loves to chew
and treats all gum as if it's new.
She sucks the flavor from every piece, then
presses it to her fleece for a later feast.
Whether it's been already chewed or already used,
terribly abused from the bottom of a shoe,
there's still a chew left for Betsie Bleu.

She chomps ten gumballs all at once,
before her breakfast and after lunch.
She chews and chews the toughest gum,
until her jaws are plum and her face feels numb.

Betsie has the record for blowing the biggest bubble.
And this is the talent that gets her into trouble.
Betsie makes bubble gum troublesome,
she just won't stop blowing them.

Betsie draws back as she takes in a long huff,
she starts to puff till she hears “That’s enough!”
Just don’t yell, “Stop!”
Or the bubble will pop,
leaving you gooey and all covered with shock.

She’s been asked to quit.
But chewing is what she loves to do,
besides blowing big bubbles that burst on you.

Simple Sally Such

Sally Such, she listened too much.
She did what she was told without a hunch.
There was just some things that you couldn't tell Sally.
She would do what she does and wouldn't find it silly.

Sally asked to be excused from the kitchen table.
She didn't feel so hungry and she just wasn't able
to eat her meat, it was way too red.
Her parents didn't think so
and sent her to bed.

"Don't come out till you're ready to eat!"
Sally listened to her parents and went to sleep.
When Sally woke up, her stomach still didn't growl.
so she crawled to the closet to play with her dolls.
Sally played and played herself back to sleep
She had been in her room fairly close to a week.

Simple Sally Such lost track of time.
She played so long it slipped her mind,
that she had to eat in order to live.
If she could have,
she should have, eaten at least one rib.

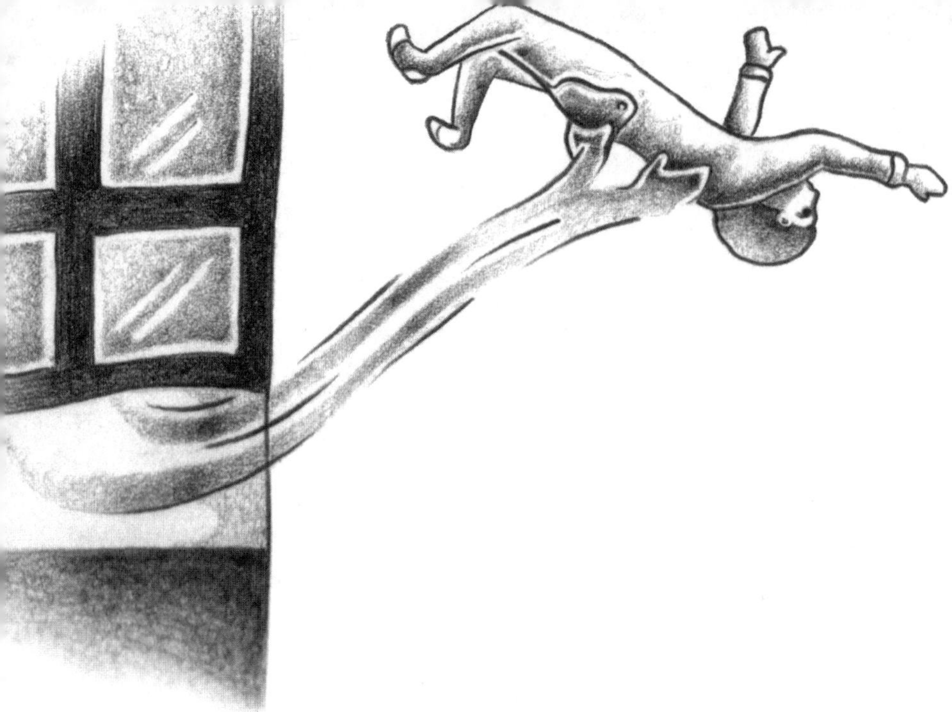

When The Wind Blows

When the wind blows at night it tickles my feet.
It gathers me up
right out of my sleep.
With a twist of my torso I'm gravity free.
Pulled from my bed, but willingly.
Around the windmill I say goodbye.
I'd rather not leave, yet I enjoy the ride.
I'm tussled, bustled and pushed through the air,
and tossed pass the trees where owl's stare.

When the winds let up
I'm rolled to the ground,
beyond the meadow to the nearest town.
Where a gust of wind flips me over the bridge,
kissing the river with slaps and kicks.
By then I'm all drenched and the wind gets cold.
Like the feel of a snowball in an ongoing throw.

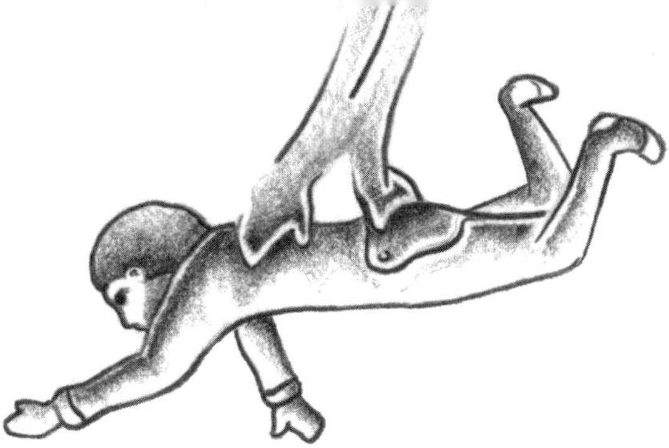

The windmill reappears, and I'm back at home.
The wind disappears and I'm on my own.
Dropped into the yard I'm fast up the stairs,
and quick to change clothes
before Mom gets there.
"There's no excuse!" she's often said.
That's true but I pledge, "I don't wet the bed."
The wind gets a little crazy.
That's all I know.
Maybe next time I'll close the window,
when the wind begins to blow.

Tea Drops

Everyone drinks the rain;
the raindrops are made of tea,

whenever the rain stops falling,
everyone's got to pee.

The Lunch Pail Thief

If you want that sandwich, you better eat up
or else you'll come back to its crumbly dust.
To leave your meal is the easiest deal
for the lunch pail thief to strike at will.
He loves sweets and tasty meats;
every lunch pail found is an artistic treat.
Whether it's pink or blue and tastes like glue,
he eats the whole thing with questionable clues.

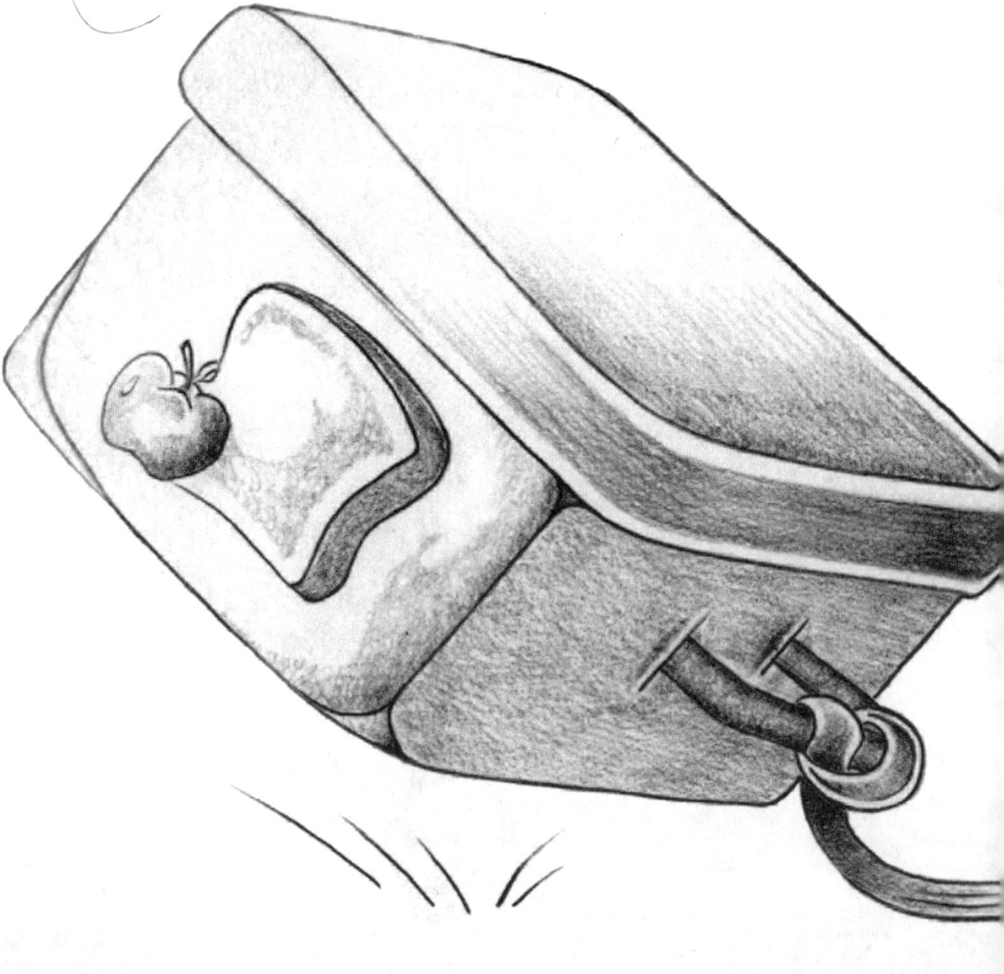

It’s incredibly frustrating without a description
besides all of the pails the kids are missing.
There haven’t been any sightings of the lunch pail thief.
There is a theory, but no belief
that the thief is nothing more
than a furry rodent.
The thought is crazy,
but trails of hairs have been noticed.
No one can see the possibility
of a small rat being the lunch pail thief.

Sal's Spot in Lunch Line

Why does Sal cut in the lunch line where I'm at?
Doesn't he know the line starts in the back?
I guess I'm pretty short, and I hardly frown.
Sal squeezes in front of me
without looking down.

Sal always waits till I get to the front.
He rudely bumps and gives out lumps
to send me flying as if I jumped
above the table where ketchup's pumped.

I'm a nice kid but enough is enough.
No more cutting on me! It's time to get rough.
I'm pushing back and it's no bluff.
I'll seem to be mean and sound really tough.

Today I tried more of a harsh appearance.
Sal knocked me beside the wall
along with my carrots.
Well I did get Sal to finally look down
reminding me why I should never frown.

When You're Tired of Everything

I'm tired of picking berries.
I'm tired of eating pears.
I'm tired of doing the same old stuff.
I feel like no one cares.

I'm tired of folding socks,
I'm tired of homework too.
I'm tired of leaving Cynthia notes;
I'm tired of thinking she's cute.

I'm tired of feeling sleepy,
I'm tired of myself.
I think I'll wrap me around a letter
and send me to someone else.

The Greatest Story Never Told

I'll tell you of a clever poem
I decided to write.

My eyelids rebelled
long hours they'd held
my first time writing at night.

My inspirations grew greater than ever.
Each idea was new.

My eyelids dropped
my pencil stopped
falling asleep halfway through...

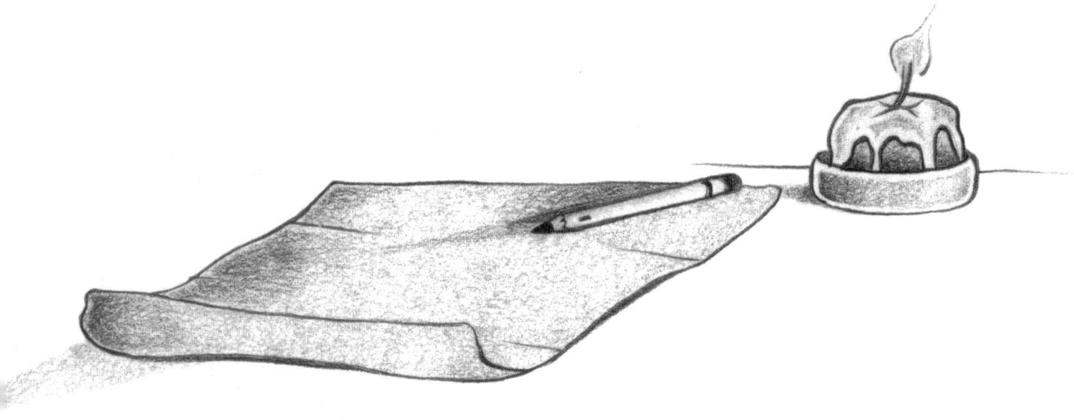

The Patient

The silly old patient was mad at me,
I refused to take out her medical IV.
Shouting on and on
the patient's mouth ran.
She didn't understand
I was just the cleaning man.
I cleaned her toilet and wiped her seat.
I went to the closet
to get fresh sheets.

The silly old patient, she still wanted more
to bring her meal and close the door,
change her gown and lotion her feet
so I suggested she wait and back I'd be.
That was the last glimpse she caught of me.

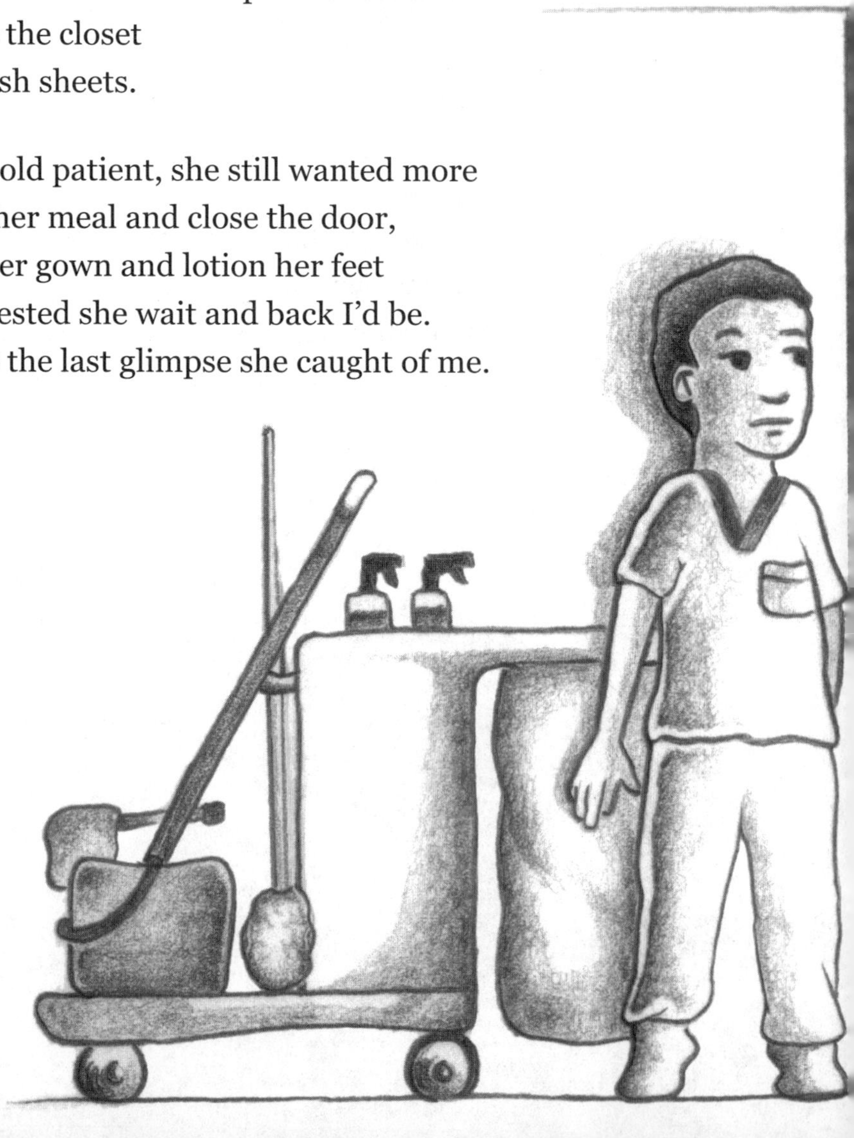

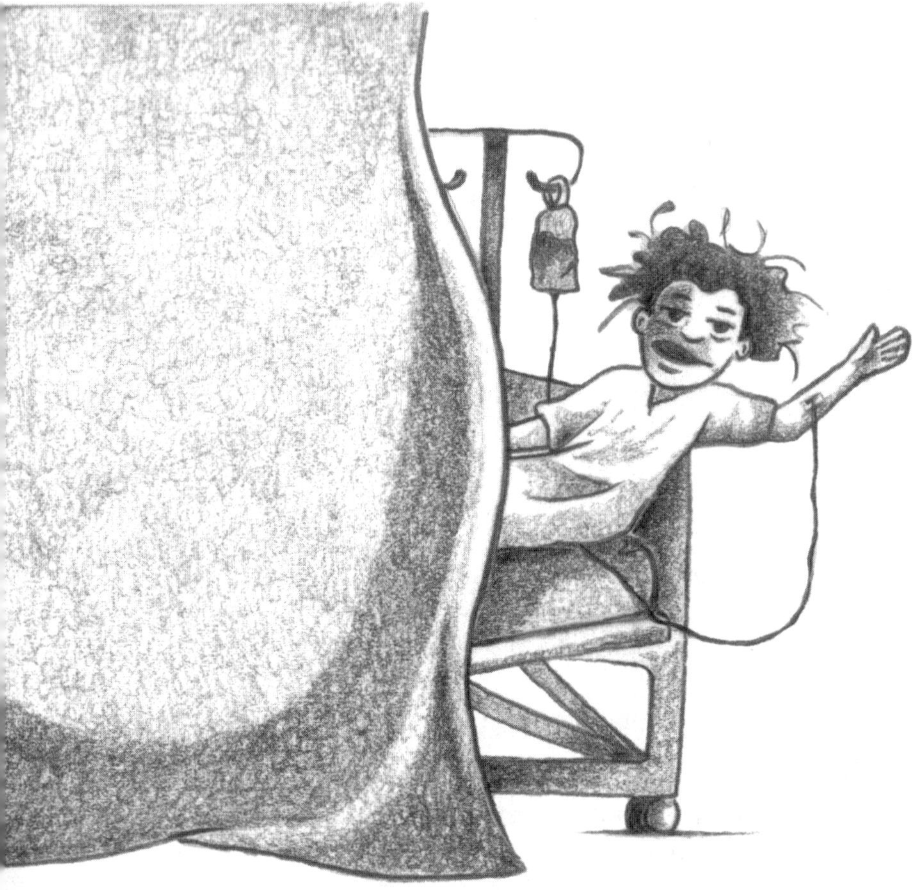

There's No Ghost!

There's a ghost in my room
I wish my parents would see.
My toys are broken,
but not because of me.

The ghost waits until I'm all alone
after Mom turns off every light in our home.
Treating my room as if it was his own,
grabbing everything that is visibly shown.

Stealing my crayons, with a silent laugh
handfuls at a time, he breaks them in half.
He's a heartless ghost without any guilt.
Though he made a mistake,
tearing my grandmother's quilt.

Jumping over the bed
I tried my hardest to snatch him.
I'll have evidence if I can just catch him.
Knocking over the dresser, smacking the floor
the ghost jumps out the window
as my parents open the door.
Without any proof my parents assume
there's no ghost in my bedroom.

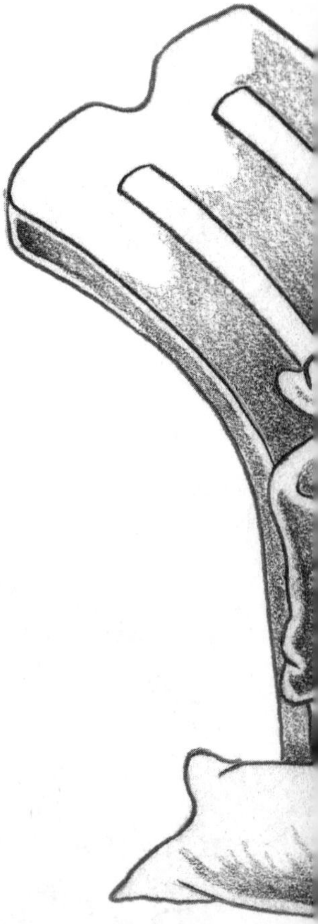

It's Okay To Smile

It's okay to smile
when I'm gone for a while
and you're not quite sure where I'm at.
It's okay to smile searching our block for a mile
while all along I was playing in the back.

It's okay to smile with your sweet tooth,
rushing home from the office late,
arriving to discover me asleep in my cover
smiling
though I ate the last piece of cake.

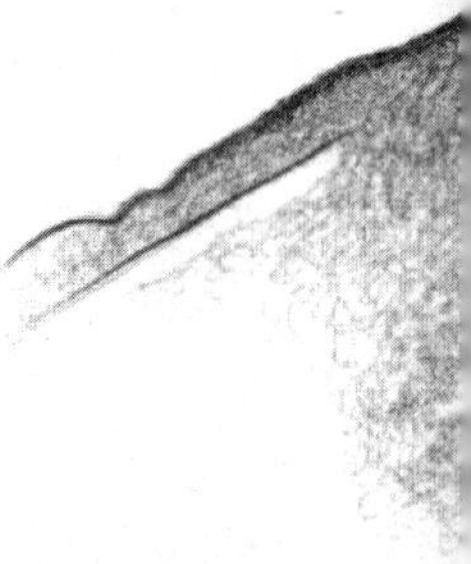

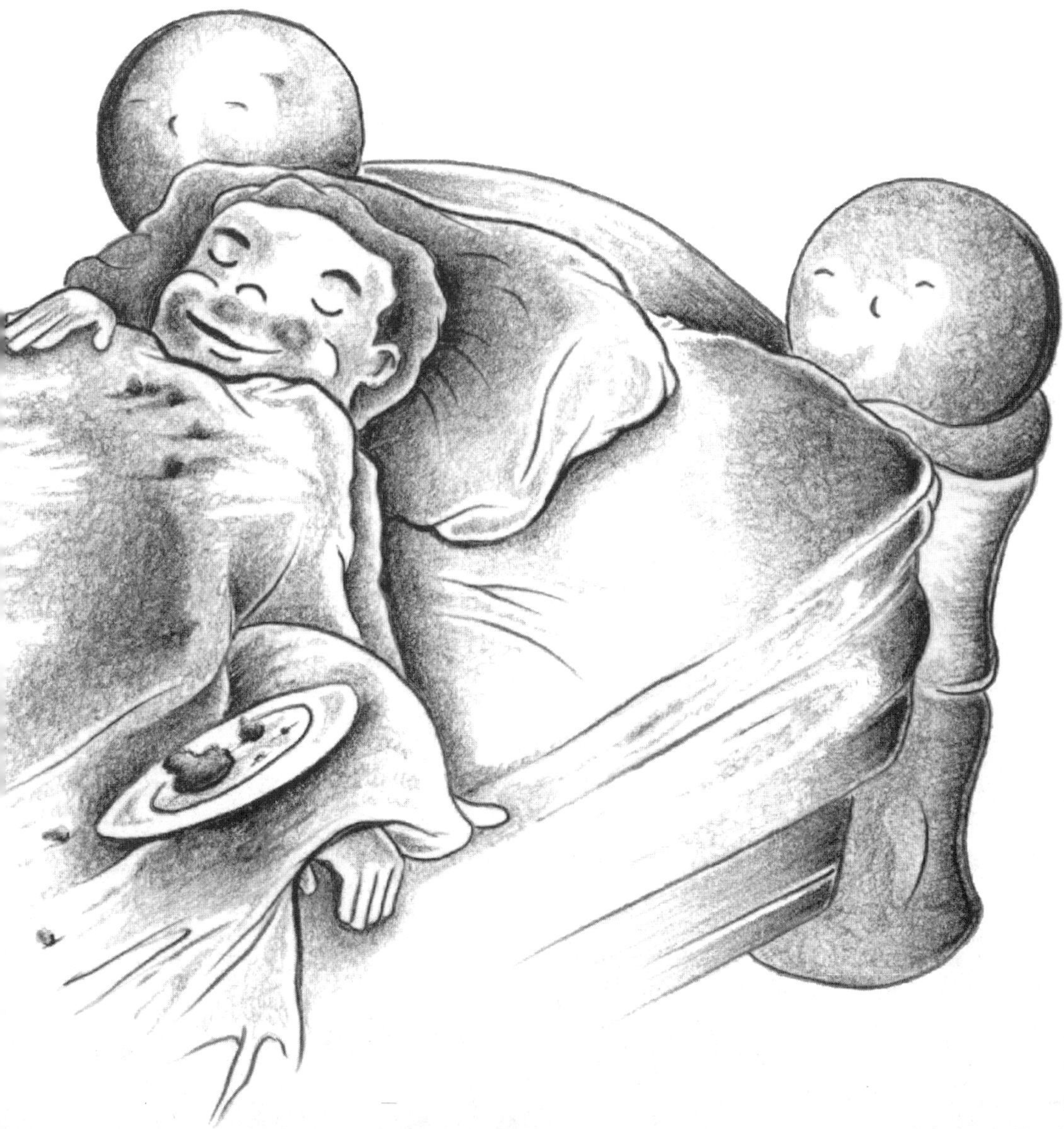

My Snowman

I have this problem
my snowman won't talk.
I've given him my boots
but he just won't walk.
He seems rather attentive with a scarf of class
I tell my best jokes
but there's no laugh.

He's firmly constructed with the finest of snow
from the top of the hill where nobody goes.
My perfect snowman is yet to show
his will to interact for his intelligence to grow.

I believe he can do it.
He just needs to prove it.
To expect one step isn't far to be fetched.
I'll give him more time
to sit still and rest.

For his day will come
to prove to us all.
He's more than a pile
of frozen snowballs.

As days become warmer
my snowman seems shorter.
More kids are outside
and their voices sound older.

Looking to my snowman
I would have never thought
that he'd choose to walk
before he decided to talk.
I heard "Watch out! Get out of the way!"
As he slipped to the ground
where his leavings still lay.

When A Kid Dreams

When A Kid Dreams

When a kid sleeps
He doesn't need to lie upon
Golden rails to dream up a castle with
candy-coated wells.
Barely a ground to doze
in the nest of peace,
just feet to walk down his road.

His imagination will take
him farther than little feet could pedal.
He doesn't need a Radio Flyer to lug his thoughts.

Just a good head on his shoulders
to carry his mind's eye.

Paradise

Does anyone know where Paradise is?
A place where we all can be pleased,
where life is a breeze and we kick with our knees
riding melons as they fall from the trees.

The air there smells like ginger.
Each inhale is a tasteful pleasure.
With just one breath the air reveals
how life is full with treasure.

It's a tropical place
where dreams are chased;
where we all have our own
with no need to race.

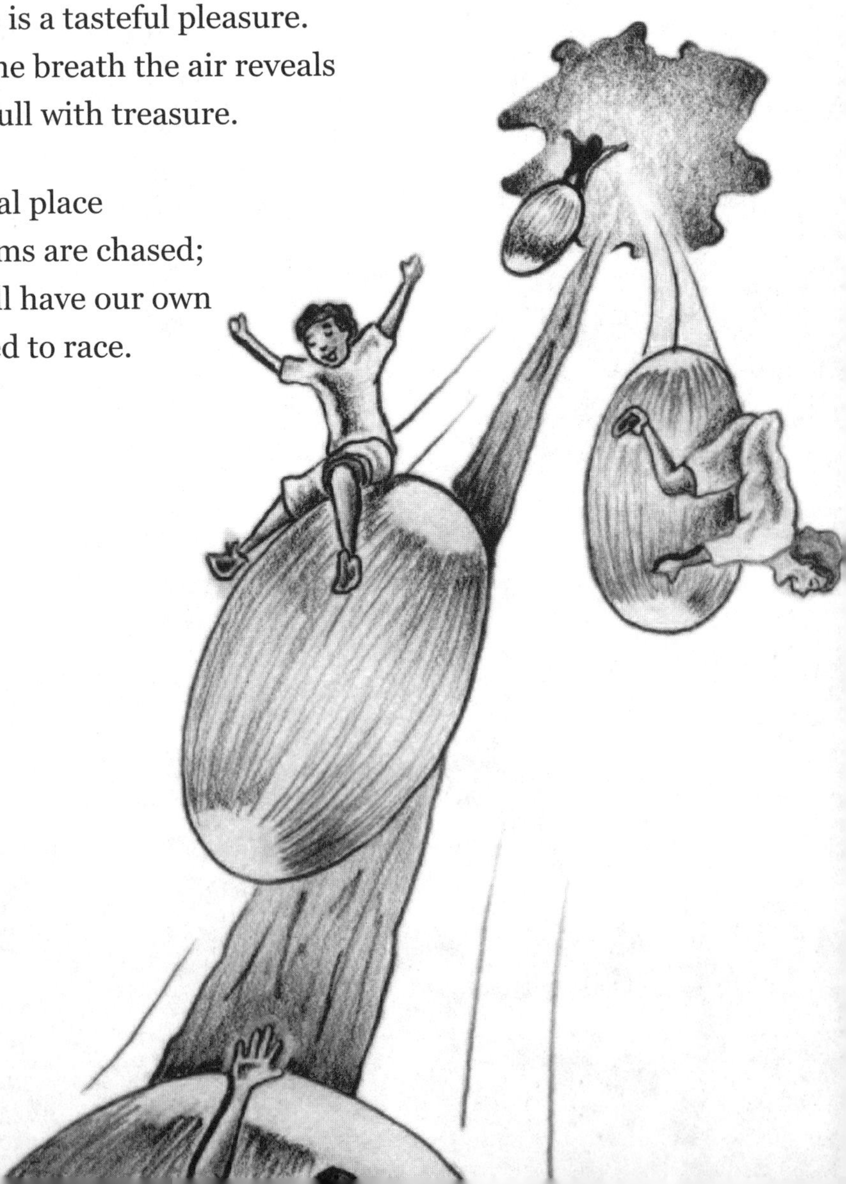

We'll lay in relaxation,
our minds overflowing with thought,
thinking of past successes and
the happiness they brought.

I'm looking around for Paradise
though it may be far away.
I'll strive everyday to be closer
if there be a cost, I'll pay.

So if anyone's planning on going,
please get tickets for two.
I'm thinking of chasing my dreams.
I'm writing down goals to pursue.

Hoops on a Tree

Basketball on a tree is an opportunity
to experience homemade fun full of festivity.
Where clothes and shoes don't make the game.
But the joy and laughter loudly exclaimed.
We dress the tree and make it more,
with chalk and plywood, Bennie keeps the score.

Though we have dirt on our faces and dust in our eyes
fun is our goal, so we improvise.
We pass and shoot, but we shoot to score.
And all day we play and forget we're poor.

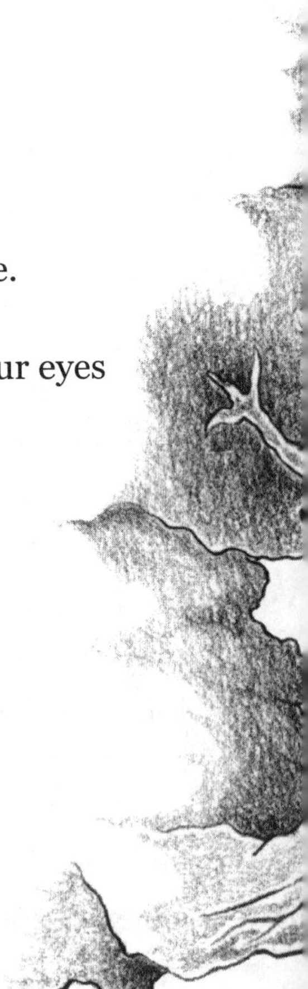

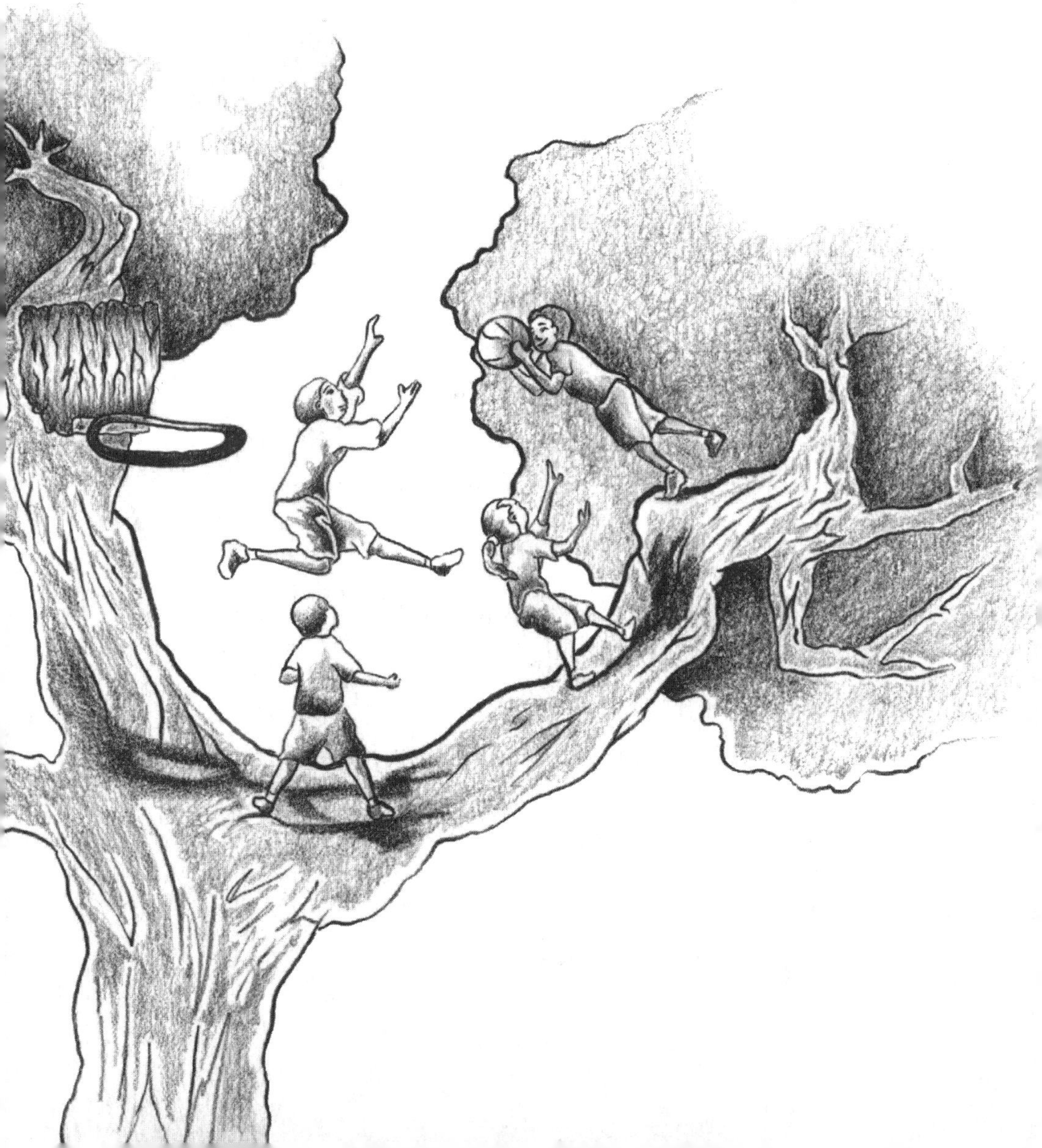

Raisins and Popcorn in a little Brown Bag

I think of my mom and what we have...
Raisins and popcorn in a little brown bag.

Though we can't afford a fixed lunch from the store,
Mom cooks me fresh popcorn so I never feel poor.
Mom shakes seasoned sprinkles into my little brown bag,
sticking to my popcorn where the butter can grab.

My little brown bag doesn't have a fancy label,
but with a marker I can write my name.
Mom gives me tiny white boxes of raisins;
they're plain, but I'm never ashamed.

Most of the kids have brand name snacks,
brand name shoes and brand name hats.
Mom sends me off with a brand new kiss every day
and I appreciate that.

Mom can't walk me to the bus stop,
she smiles telling me to be careful.
Often times I feel afraid,
but I hear Mom's voice say, "Be prayerful."

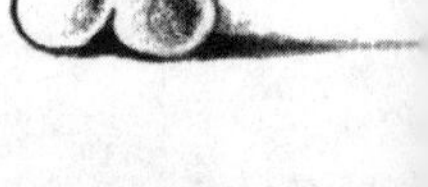

Mom doesn't always have much.
But Mom doesn't ever feel sad.
Mom gives me all of what she has...
raisins and popcorn in a little brown bag.

Away in the Mirror

I stare at my missing tooth
fallen,
to be replaced by another.
Dad says, "One day it'll be gone for good
it won't come back and that's just that."

How can something you love and see everyday,
leave to never return?

I brush my teeth and smile at them.
I appreciate each tooth,
each parent.
I love my mom, I kiss her
like my tooth one day I'll miss her.

Free Lemonade!

No one knows why Tyler's Lemonade is made.
He'll pour you a glass even if he's not paid.
An icy cold lemon in each sip to the lip
sends the hottest summer day away on a trip.
It tastes the best. It's truly divine.
He could make a trillion dollars if he had the mind.

Tyler's lemonade stand is beneath a tree.
Covered in shade he's proud to be,
the only lemonade stand where the drink is free
where his cardboard sign reads, "Come on up, it's on me."
He knows that if he keeps giving his reward will come.
Someone will honor him for the deeds he has done.

Indeed a man walked up in a luxurious suit,
that complemented the bright light that shined from his shoe.
The gentleman grinned as he reached for his pocket
and pulled out a check attached to a golden locket.
The man paid Tyler and left with a smile.
Tyler wanted to thank him but didn't know how.
He accepted the check but felt a bit nervous,
until he saw that his check read, "Community Service."

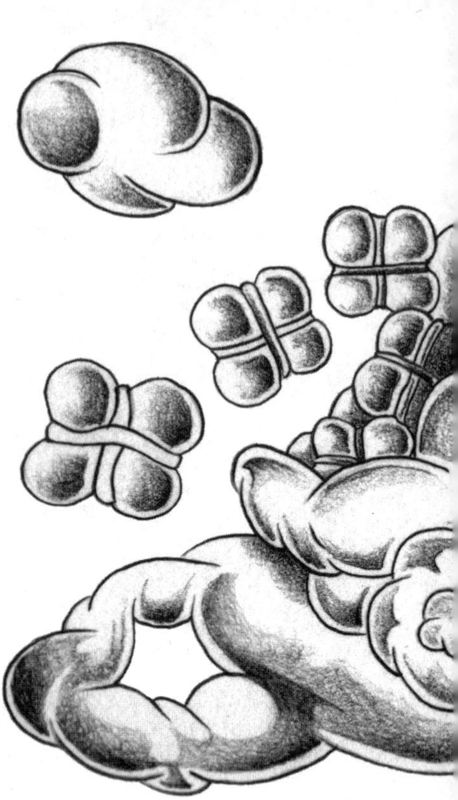

Things A Kid Shouldn't Be Told!!!

Don't work so hard getting your hopes up!

Build your hopes so high to the sky the
clouds invite your dreams inside.
Grabbing, holding, tucking and molding fabricated scenes,
along the air without despair
the clouds will model your dreams.

That takes a lot though!

I like lump sums, big trucks carrying tons
to my home where I can fiddle.
It takes a lot to get a lot,
raise your hand if you want a little.

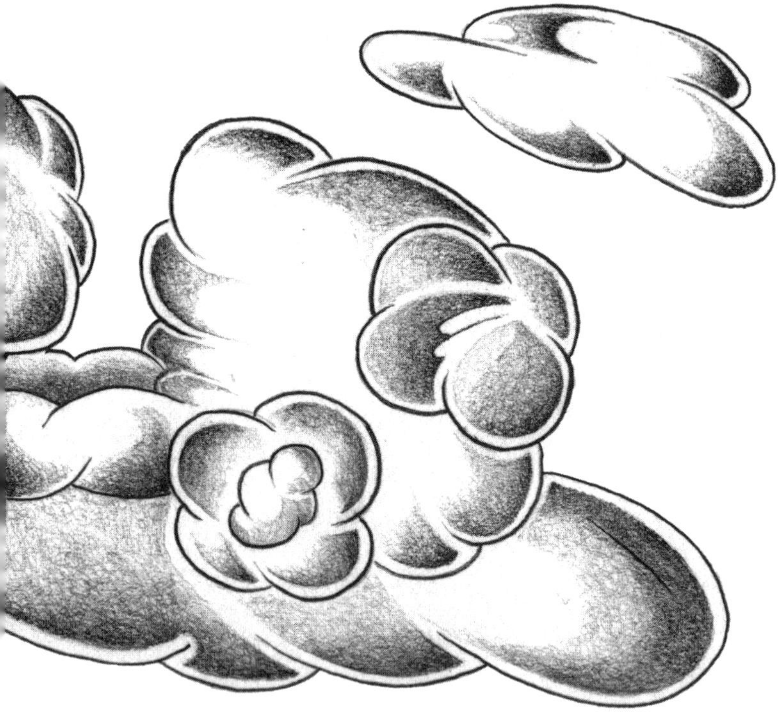

Don't forget where you come from!

If it's great to stay focused on where you're going,
why spend so much time where you're at?
If the past hasn't been real pleasant to live,
why remember that?

Some choose to forget where they came from,
when environments aren't so good.
Thanks for the respect
but don't expect,
for me to say whether or not you should.

A Special Gift to You

It's Christmas time, but I don't want much
just my family and I all bunched up
in our cozy little cottage, lit by a single flame
having fun playing our traditional game
though we play it every year, it's never the same.

We talk tall talk as we fill our tummies
with sugary treats and softly Gummies.
We love to share and give great gifts
and hope each gift will help uplift
the thought that counts which finishes the quiz
and answers the question of what Christmas is.

We don't only exchange the gifts that tarnish.
We share our worlds, and bless he who has brought us.
We meet, eat and greet with treats,
so why not make Christmas every day of the week?
Who says you can't? In our cottage we do.
First give your life the gift of you.

You’re invited to our cottage to look about.
Knock on the door and joy will come out.
It’s our present to you and it’s no loan.
Now hurry off quickly to carry it home.
Wrap it around your heart, curve and bend.
And just wait, you’ll see
someone wants to come in.

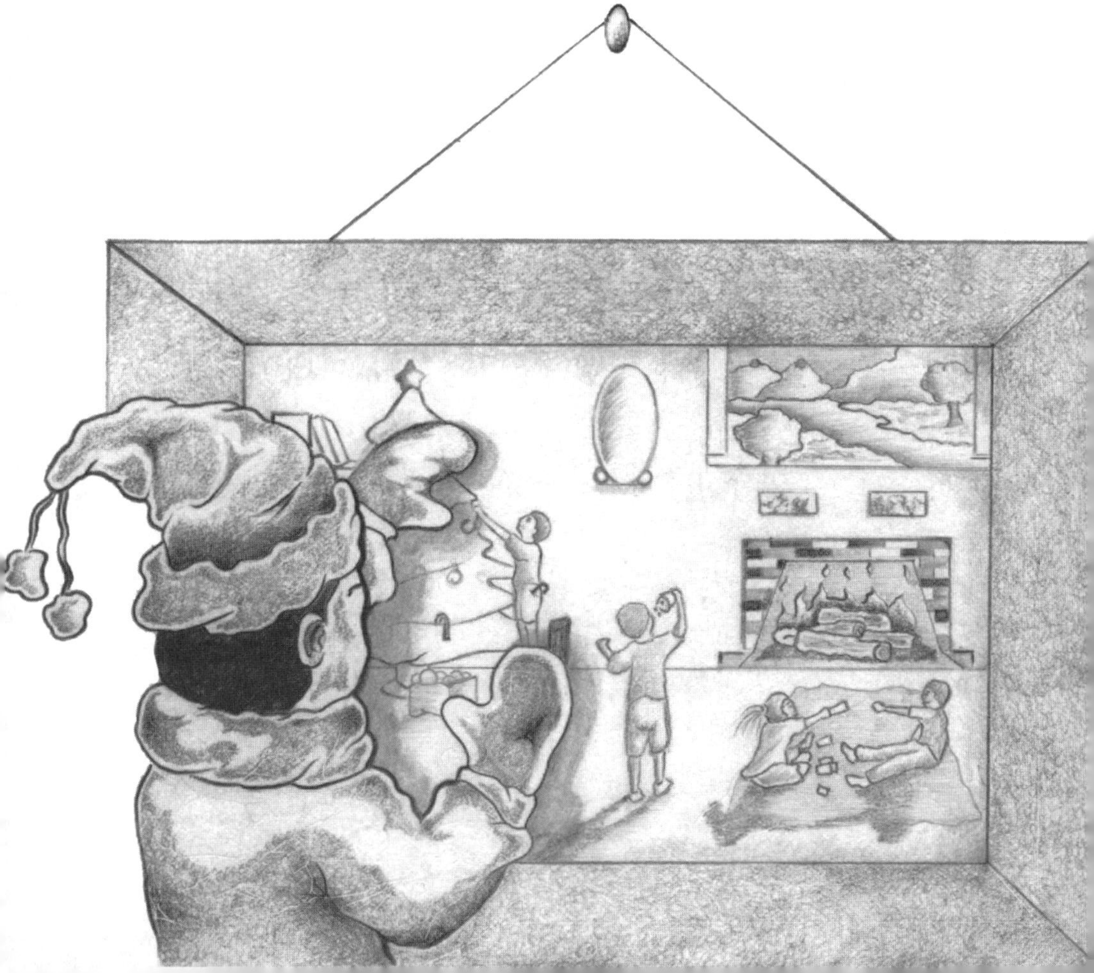

Life In A Bag

It's been scattered around;
my life in a bag,
mixed with dreams
I'd love to have.

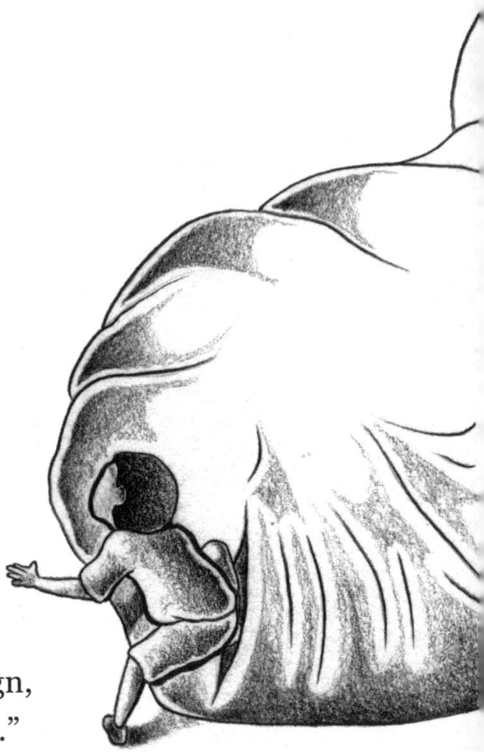

Though my eyes can't speak,
my voice will hum.
And every now and then
yup, dreams do come.
And when they do each one's a big sign,
"Life is more than one single file line."

So yes! I'm in a bag with a double tied knot,
still
I'll climb to the top and imagine I'm not.
I'll dream of places far from this bag
within a blue and pink sky where cotton is dragged.
And if dreaming is hope, then my life's not through.
I'm making it work--like grandma said--when she used to.

And when I'm out, I'll live to be me;
The only little kid who makes me free.
I won't be sad when my eyelids sag,
I'll dream me gone away from this bag.

Liberty's Hands

Once you hid me away in your cellar
where you thought I'd lose my pride.
Physically in darkness
beneath wooden doors
but mentally alive outside.

I can't explain how I made it
such lonely hope I had.
You attacked my inner person
your intentions of one less lad.

Through all my hardships, I never gave in.
Much light shined through the doors.
Too many dreams and sight within,
they'll never live under your floor.

Now it's much too late, they're above your gates
and out from the stretch of your land.
They glide the greenest hilltops
where they stand in Liberty's hands.

DREAMS

The Wall of Many Dreams

I have discovered the wall of infinite dreams
where true dreams come alive.
Whatever I think is there in a blink
of a grin within my eyes.

I can see my dreams across the wall
welcoming to my reach.
Stretching tall against the wall
it's rather hard to speak.

Families are there, dreaming together.
No one's dream is seen by another.
I've seen my dream house
with a picket fence
and without the worries of the landlord's rent.

I went to a friend to share the wall,
of my infinite dreams of which I had saw.

She didn't believe me, but still she came
again my dreams appeared the same.

She stared for minutes, but "Nothing" she claimed.
She walked away not even ashamed.

My friend must have had no dreams at all,
until she told me,
I didn't know there were bricks on the wall.

DREAMS

Everyone Wins

Little Stan Has a Plan

Little Stan is a future star.
He keeps his posture up to par.
He encourages other kids to stay on track.
He's creative in areas his peers lack.
Wherever he goes he leaves a print
as a memoir of how his time is spent.
Stan hopes his motto will help kids follow
his prints to plan their every tomorrow.

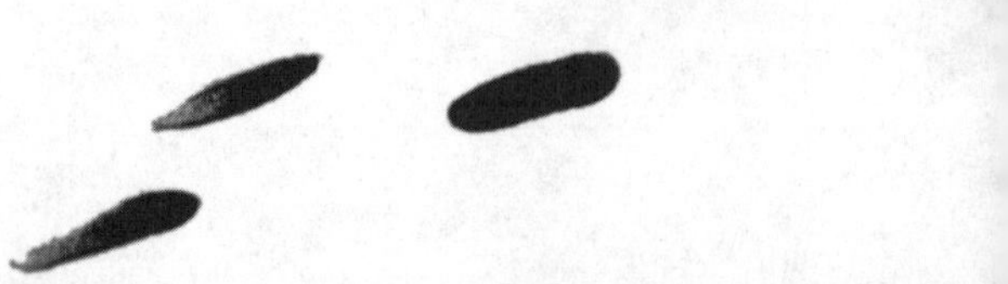

The Innovative Faucet

Ivan the Inventor invented an inventor
to invent an innovative faucet.
For people with flies, skeletons, and lies
tucked in their little secret closets.

It washes away guilt and shame
and pours out love like April's rain.
It do's all the does that water do.
That's exactly what it does,
it waters you!
You'll grow a happy life
cause after all life is nice;
when it's clear as if you lived it twice.
You'll say, "This's great!" You can't help but mention,
giving thanks to Ivan's inventor's invention.

Your Choice!

When you truly invest
you choose to be rich.
Every morning you wake up
you decide what you get.
If you go to the gym
it's your choice to be fit.
Once you realize these principles
your dreams are legit.

If you see what you want
it's possible to reach
when applying your mind
and moving your feet.

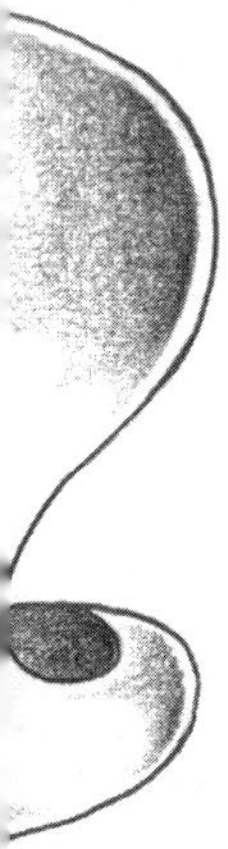

Prove you want to move
and stop standing still.
Few eat in the restaurant
without paying the bill.
Roll down your eyelids and watch your thoughts cruise.
Unless you quit, you never lose.
So make your choice and choose your goals.
One step toward the Sun, is a foot from the cold.

The Day I Found Out Who I Was

Today I had fallen deep asleep
and realized that there were two of me.

Me was meek but I was more show.
They both wanted to stay, so neither would go.

For once I got quiet to let Me speak.
He said,
"You are strong when I am weak."

"You open doors that close on Me.
I'm the lock and you're the key."

All along I was only fighting Me.

I started slow in the race of life.
Me never went fast so I had it nice.
I is a champion in every race he's in
since I got out of the way to let Me win.

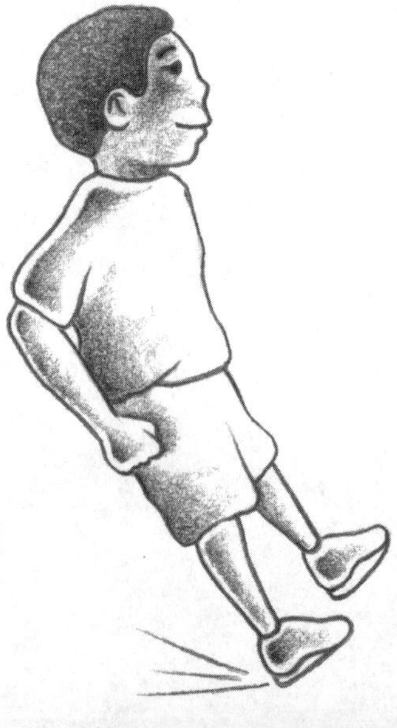

If the Kids Keep Their Secret

If the kids keep their secret
we can smile and watch them grow.
If the kids keep their secret
when their parents tell them no.

If the kids keep their secret
with no pen to write a poem.
If the kids keep their secret
when Santa skips their home.

If the kids keep their secret
while homework seems extreme.
If the kids forget the shabby peers
and still decide to dream.

If the kids keep their secret
they won't have to tell a soul.
For anyone who watches them
will know that they have goals.

I Met A Word

I wanted to be heard and searched for a word.
That word I found was success.

We sat and made a pact together,
that we'd both give our best.

Success had taught me
how to work
like hard-hat men
with flannel shirts.

For each of the soup kitchens with kittens, we cleaned
there was dirt to be done, but good to be gleaned.

We tiptoed through stress holding on to our best,
in the midst of a mess-covered floor.
And all through the rubbish, brown-reddish
wet lettuce, success had given me more.

We learned and taught.
Talked and walked,
realizing that we were our best.
We danced our dance and pranced a prance
in honor of night's lost rest.

So we laughed and played
after the price we paid,
sitting with success on a pact we made.

For Those I Love

It's a fight when I write
there's so much I could say
I've learned so much
more than I knew yesterday.

Through all the tests that birthed success
so many wonderful people I think of...
I exhale and smile for who I am
as I write for those I love.

Perfect People

I thought I was the only one
who messed up more than once
Who tripped and fell,
~~misspelled~~ and yelled, "Boy am I a Dunce!"
I figured that I was the only one
who forgot great words to say.
But we all at times misplace our minds
like a scarecrow loses hay.
I thought that being "Perfect"
was based on a perfect life,
but anyone who is someone
has messed up more than twice.

Portrait

You can never impress everyone
regardless of how hard you try.
It's obvious you're not perfect
though have you asked yourself why?

You can paint a pretty picture
bright, or maybe blue.
Does that make the painting a picture of you?
If it's not a self-portrait,
maybe it's an inside of you picture.
For every brush stroke there's a new adventure.

So if you paint really fast, but consciously
it's a masterpiece of you, accept it to be.
Once the canvas is dry and the painting is through
open your eyes and let your painting sketch you.

Portraits are painted for revenue.
If you see yourself a winner, you never lose.
Paint yourself with colorful hues
and when rainbows shine
you'll see a portrait of you.

Care Free

Suspended through the air causing a draft.
Innocent trees enjoying my laugh.
It's a happy free laugh.
A "be proud of me" because "I'm about to be" laugh.

Flying through dreams as the winds kick my feet
holding onto my swing sitting high in my seat.
Enjoying my life for all that it is.
Thankful to friends who make life easier to live.

I find much delight in my swing set.
Within it there's so much light I won't forget

how free I feel without regret.

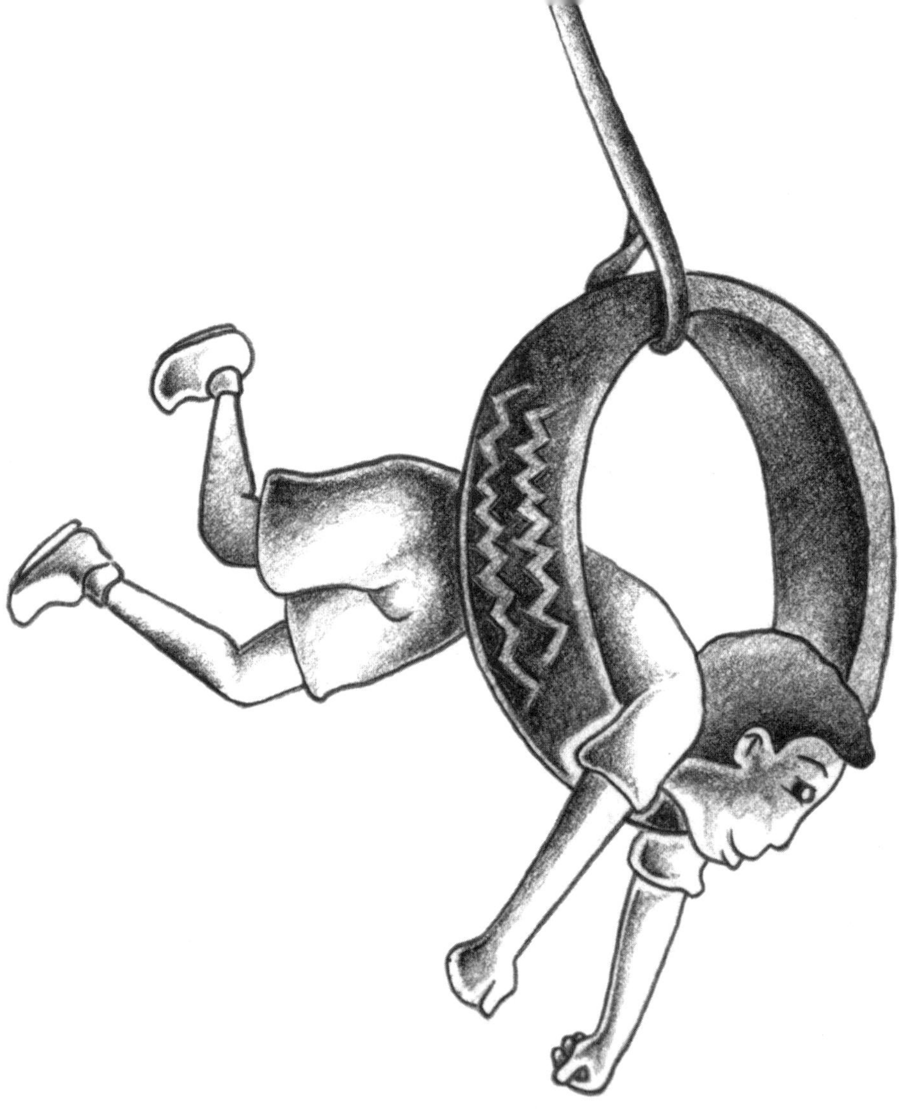

Come With Me

Let's go outside to enjoy a beat.
We can be happy kids and run the streets.

Maybe we should stay in to avoid the heat
and wrestle Grandpa off of his feet.
If he gives us change to buy a treat
we could run off to fetch a truck of sweets.

Just our luck, "It's the Ice Cream Truck!"
The kids are swarming, "Let's hurry up!"

From around the corner it comes on leisure
full of ice cream bars dancing inside the freezer.
If we have enough we can get a giant popsicle
or settle for smaller if our desire is little.

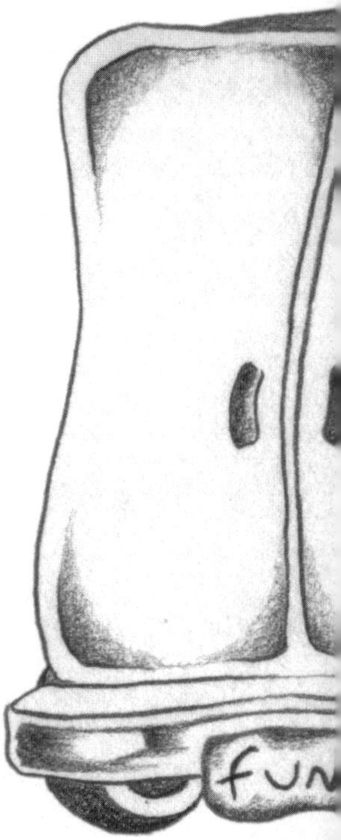

The ice cream man waves till he's off
as he turns the corner to attract another brawl.

If you're not tired yet, we can follow that sound.
The laughter of kids at our favorite playground.
Where we all yell with our outside voices
enjoying the freedom of our everyday choices.

Everyone Wins

If everyone believed that everyone wins,
then everyone receives because everyone lends.
Just think of the joy our world would be in
a world of success without any end.

Where everyone put in what everyone takes.
So everyone eats, but everyone bakes.
Everyone cares and everyone shares.
If anyone's in need, everyone spares.

When everyone buys what everyone sells
everyone has and everyone's well.
If everyone listens to everyone's tales
everyone's humble when everyone yells.

If everyone loves and everyone mends
no one ever loses because everyone wins.

The Greatest Jump by Susie Stump

Susie Stump, she loves to jump.
Susie falls, she gets back up.

She jumps so high she dropkicks the sky
even hopes one day she soon will ride
a shooting star when caught in sight
and just this night
she caught her flight.

With a single leap Susie was far from here,
in the domain of a star-spangled atmosphere.
Where she found her star that shined bright
and took her for her famous flight.

She joined the star through space's massive maze
and scoped several planets from far away.

The star slowly dropped with Susie Stump
who couldn't believe The Amazing Jump
she executed because her hopes were up.

It's Going Somewhere

Look at that Ball, it's going somewhere.
I can't tell you where but far from here.
With its attractive roll and glamorous flare
I tell you that Ball is going somewhere.

It'll ride the hilltops to gain momentum
then cruise the valleys to explore what's in them.

Please don't try to stop it. You'll just lose your hair.
I tell you that ball is going somewhere.

The Girl Who Flew

You've heard of the boy who could fly
but what of the girl who flew.
She felt her dream was a bit extreme
so there wasn't many who knew.

She loved her dream so much
she kept her head to the sky
and even though she had to wake up
she never forgot how to fly.

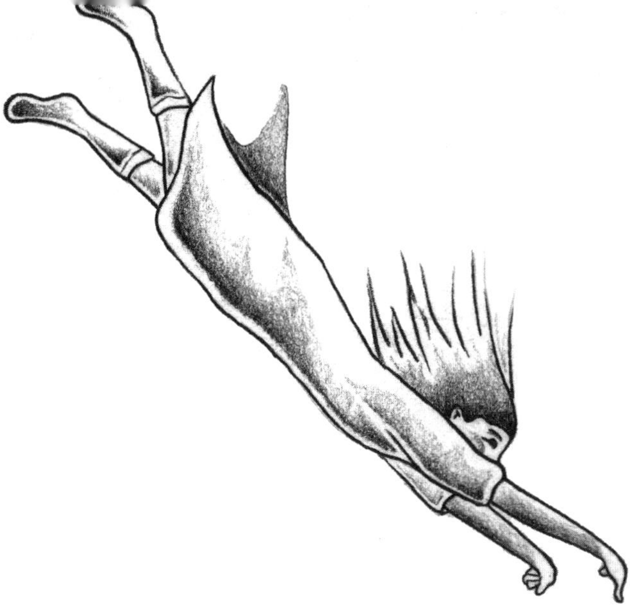

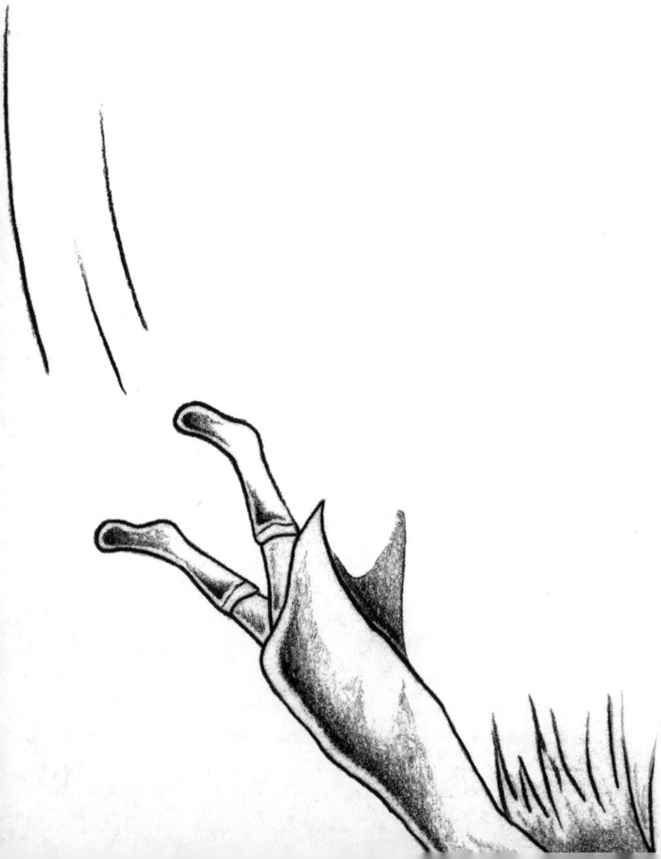

When Inspiration Gets Out

The Books Are Flying Away

Please don't leave me ignorant
and take your words away.
I'll read you more and more each day,
just promise that you'll stay.

I can reach the cookies in the wooden cupboard
but still I need to grow.
I realize the fact that you're what I lack
and full of what I don't know.

From under my bed, out of the shed
each note and every letter;
I'll read while riding on the bus
sniffling from winter's weather.

Now that you have my attention,
I'll love the words you say,
If you'll turn around,
drop your bags, and promise that you'll stay.

Home for a Poem?

I'm a Poem without a home. Do you know of a place?
Where I can be read and tears can be shed to spread a little faith.
A big house is great, but a shelter would do fine.
Just somewhere to lay this letter of mine.

For the generous being who provides a home
will receive much more than a thankful Poem.
But an everlasting fire that lights your wick
to lessen the drips of your candlestick.

Inside your home I'll give a loving lecture
and fill each room with laughter's pleasure.
I'll roam your home till I find the phone,
clean the speaker and check the tone.
So this one Poem has a gorgeous home.

A Wisdom Note To Self

An apple is just a fruit until it's bitten.
A thought is just an idea until it's written.

A shoe is just a shoe until it's worn.
A promise is just a promise until it's sworn.

A bottle is just a container until it's filled.
A testimony is just a secret until it's revealed.

Illustrate your thoughts to bring more of you out.
Sow your seeds in a place where they'll sprout.
A lively garden will cast away doubt.

No Title, No Limits

Please.........

Don't give me a short title bound by its walls.
With its limits on what I can or can't scrawl.
I'll cross the perimeter.
I'll surpass with a blast,
cracking its structure made of fool's glass.

So go ahead and give me your titles,
as if I've asked.
For the final time I'll inform you,
they're not going to last.

The Time I Forgot How to Fall

I think of when I was twelve, I used to fall a lot.
I learned to skate on brand new blades
and never wanted to stop.
A Band-Aid here and a Band-Aid there
with skin to spare the price was fair.

Years Passed....

I began to skate well, and well I did.
I'd spin in circles and backwards uphill.
Clenching my knees, wrestling the wind's hair,
defying gravity as viewers stared.

Years Passed....

The pavement lost the taste of my skin,
and stayed beneath my feet.
With an awkward spin we met again
as I tripped from a crack in the street.

This fall was different
the pain has come inside.
It entered my leg and passed my thigh
upset my stomach
and scraped my pride.

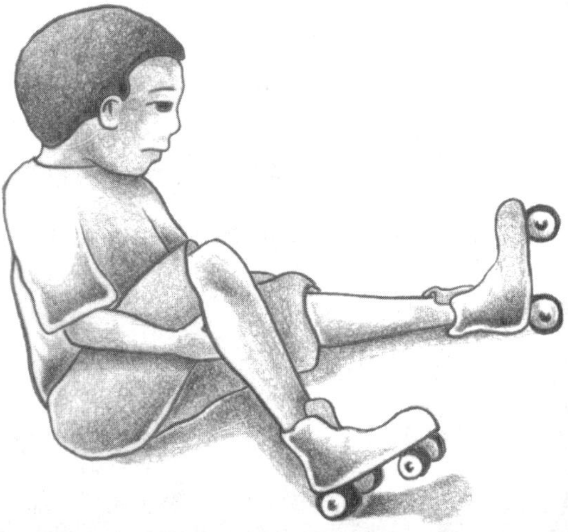

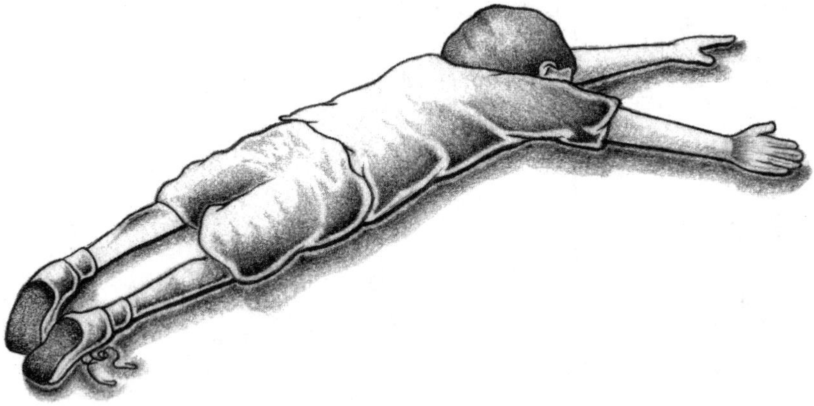

In Cases of Emergency

For tornadoes we close the windows.
For fires we close the doors.
What'll we do when everything's closed,
and emergencies are out of control?
If you want me to lie
I'll sit and try
to lie across the floor and wait to die.

My Room's No Walk in the Park

The light in my room is out.
It's a shame that my room gets dark.
Daytime we have sun and at night the moon,
so it should be a walk in the park.
My room can be quite eerie
when the sun has gone away.
So at night I sit in my windowsill
and beg the moon to stay.

The Stars at Night

The stars at night leave, but they always come back.
Like my great Uncle Jim who leaves his hat.
Stars are good days that seem so rare.
Aligned like Grandpa sitting still in his chair.

The stars at night are here even in the day.
The lack of sight makes them so far away.
Where night once fell, the Cocks awake.
The nightly stars disappear
as dawn decides to break.

The stars at night wait on us to see if we'll wait for them.
Even though they're often forgotten
they come back time and again.
Be sure to show them attention
and welcome them everywhere you're at.
For our stars at night leave
but they always seem to come back.

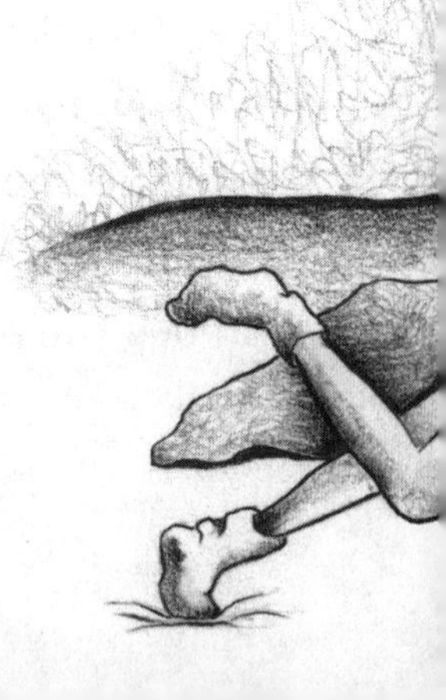

Sight or Vision?

What's the pleasure of sight without vision?
Isn't it a gift to live and have both? Or,
does one cancel the other out, like
a liar under oath?

Though unable to see, it's not stressful for me
I thank God I know where I'm going.
I vision myself on sunny billows, till
someone with sight says it's snowing.

Through city gates and town estates
my ears can't bare the sight.
The greed of fools on evening news
I pray for their vision each night.
If what I hear is our world today
Lord, keep my sight and take it away.

Sight, or vision?
One, or the other?
Well don't be surprised of which I'd choose
after hearing you use,
your words when you speak about color.

Where the Sun Reaches the Oak

When the massive Oak towers my presence
I stand rejected by light.
The Oak never moves
so I have to choose
which ways are left and right.

I search for clarity to bring forth vision
to escape the shadow in which I'm living.
This time I'm leaving; I'm gone for good.
Never mind understanding what can't be understood.

I could climb over
though I've tried that before.
My heart was willing,
but my hands were too sore.

When the Oak's bark sheds,
it falls from the sky
making it harder to leave without asking why.
"I've been here before" and now I recall
what I've done in the past
to reach the light that I saw.

Always at this moment the sun tickles a limb
as a clue of which direction I'm to walk in.
Just when darkness grabs for my throat
I see the other side where the sun reaches the Oak.

Questions?

Sometimes I wonder why the sun comes up...
Why the darkness turns to light?

How come...
When the Eagle brushes the air in flight
I join its journey, but only through sight?

How come moods change like a clock on the wall?
Why one person, one way
affects us all.

Why do so many people agree
with so many things that feel wrong?
How come no one sings together,
one great big song?

How do you find answers for the unanswered questions?
You know,
the ones not covered
through the course of school lessons.

Shall I forget my posture in my premature age?
Thus, demanding my answers through an
immature rage?
Or will I hold them in, hoping to grow old and wise,
seeing the world with everyone else's eyes?

As a kid being bold I'm often told
that, "Some questions will always remain."
If that's the truth, when I grow up
maybe then,
I'll say the same.
But that's hard to accept,
by the kid who wept
from his dreams being hit by a plane.

An Angel's Kiss

Last night I kissed an Angel
inside in my little home.
Beside my broken fireplace
I thought that I was alone.

In the midst of grief I found relief
when finally looking above.
Feeling grace against my face
I embraced my greatest hug.

All of the good memories lightened the room
rebuilt from the hearth
where they once were consumed.
Smiles made their way back with aspiring bliss
as I sat in the arena of an Angel's kiss.

The Boy Who Hid In His Hair

The boy who hid in his hair,
he thought that no one cared.
He tucked in his pride with his dreams inside
because no one ever taught him to share.

The boy grew tall on his feet
his hair was short of his ears.
He experienced things that he'd never seen
and finally done away with his fear.

But the boy blew his last little tire
wondering who could possibly ever care.
God seeing a perfect opportunity,
opened his trunk and provided a spare.

Have Half

Is it true you're so hungry that you can't even laugh?
I've got a sandwich full of jokes
and you're welcome to half.
The shorting of your blanket allows a brisk draft.
Mine is comfortably large,
please enjoy half.

Everywhere you go you go as half.
So when you go
you're always last.
To be complete
you'll need another.
Take half from me, it's whole forever.

If you won't take half then what will you do?
We all need tools
with bolts and screws,
shiny days and gigantic moons.
But Still!
Oh still!
You're not convinced
that half from me is without rent.
No bond, no strings, no catch attached.
Have half of me to help relax.

You're the yoke of my egg,
the sugar for my spice.
Some cakes you'll never bake
without having half twice.

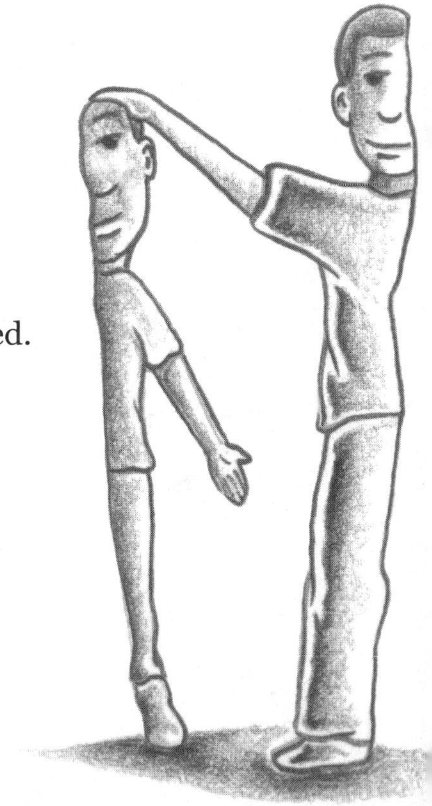

My Cup of Tea

You're not
a foreign language, or difficult to learn.
You're
butter across my French bread,
and utterly churned.
You don't
change colors like the leaves in the fall.
More so, you run your same pattern without dropping the ball.

You're
one rare white rose in a bed of red,
unique and gorgeous through each season's shed.

Your water-colored eyes wet the crescent of my smile.
They strengthen my love with impressionable style.

I could go on forever so I'll sum it up...

The sky would fall into pieces
trying to hold up what you are to me.

But,
if you were to shrink into a drink...

you'd be my cup of tea.

Missing Pieces

There are pieces missing in me.
Pieces that I must find.
Just give me a minute
to search myself.
So life will once again shine.

Great fun! There's one.
Ooh Ooh! There's two.
Two more and I'm through.
No fear there here.
Look there, it's a pair!
Such pleasure, so sweet
my life is complete.

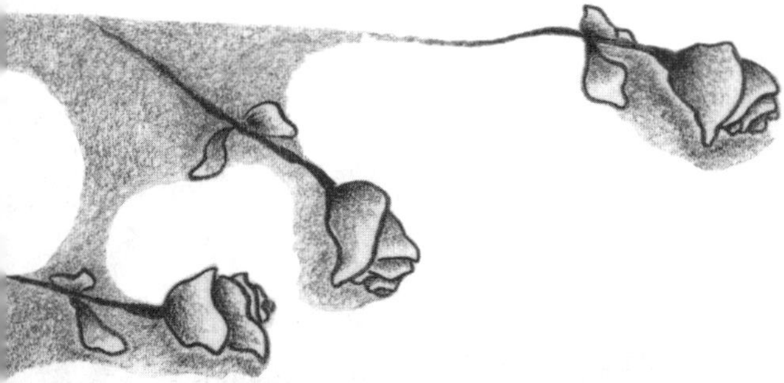

When Inspiration Gets Out

Inspiration comes from within
and that I do not doubt.
I went to the park just today
and mine has walked right out.

Inspiration sat on the seesaw in the middle of the park
up and down, smile and frown looking for a heart.
When discouragement went up, Inspiration came down.
Inspiration left to ride the merry-go-round.
Nothing went up and nothing came down
things stayed the same,
just around and around.

Inspiration approached the slide,
climbed up, but slid back down
losing hope and ready to leave
but the jungle gym was found.
Inspiration climbed its way to the top
smiling while leaving the ground,
laid its back against the bars
and never came back down.

Bye!

A Little bit about Joshua...

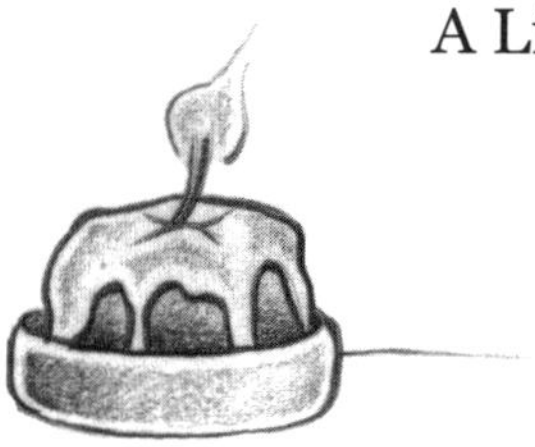

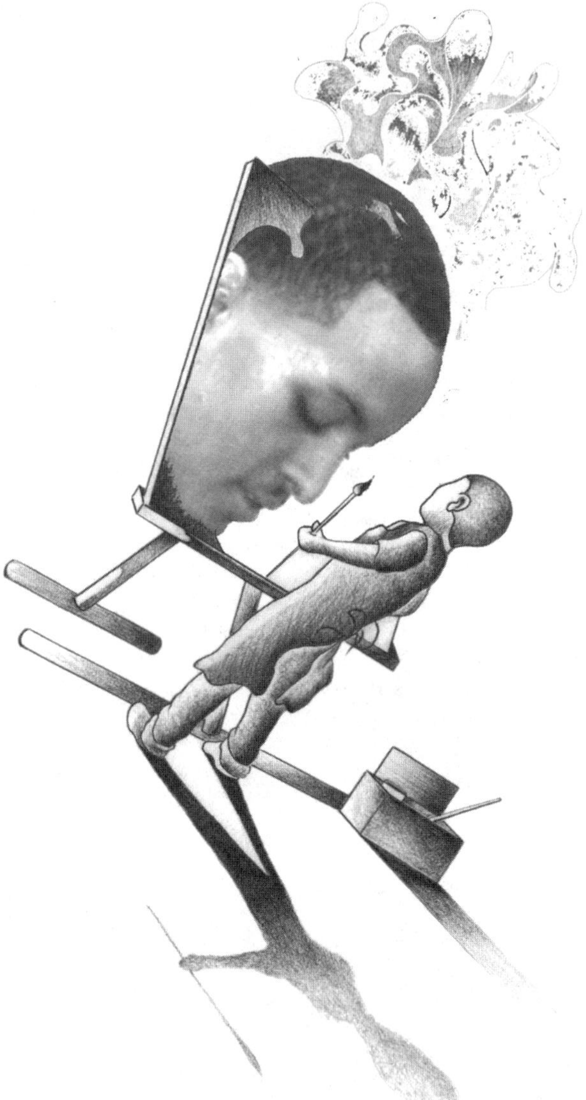

Joshua earned his Bachelors Degree in Fine Arts from the University of Michigan. He works as the creative coordinator for Zoe Life Publishing. He currently lives in Ypsilanti, Michigan with his wife Kenya. Joshua enjoys attending church, reading, writing, drawing, playing basketball, table tennis, and singing in the shower.

Great people do great things
for other people who don't feel so great.
It's like making a difference in someone's life
you didn't know God would soon take.

Great people don't settle for anything less
than their best
and you know who you are.
Ordinary people who run their race
whether with bus fare or a car.

Great people create great books of pathways they took
hoping that others come along.
They encourage you to write them too
so
whoever says you're not great will be wrong.

Other Books For Children Published by Zoe Life Publishing